Patsy Cline

CRAZY FOR LOVING YOU

Published on the occasion of the exhibition
Patsy Cline: Crazy for Loving You

Country Music Hall of Fame® and Museum

Opening August 2012

With an essay by Paul Kingsbury

Foreword by Rosanne Cash

COUNTRY MUSIC FOUNDATION PRESS
Nashville, Tennessee
2012

COUNTRY MUSIC FOUNDATION PRESS

222 Fifth Avenue South • Nashville, Tennessee 37203

(615) 416-2001

978-0-915608-11-9

This publication was created by the Staff of the Country Music Hall of Fame® and Museum.

Editors: Mick Buck and John W. Rumble

Printer: Lithographics, Inc., Nashville, TN

Except where otherwise credited, images in this book come from the collection of the Country Music Hall of Fame® and Museum.

Introduction

Since 1967, the Country Music Hall of Fame® and Museum has used many strategies to carry out its mission of preserving the evolving history of country music and educating its audiences. In addition to museum exhibits, our school and public programs, CD and DVD reissues, Web site, and publications help us reach fans, students, scholars, and members of the music industry, in Nashville and around the world. This companion book for *Patsy Cline: Crazy for Loving You*, like the exhibit, continues to fulfill our overarching goals.

In planning the book, our museum staff decided to offer readers a publication that would supplement—but not duplicate—the exhibit itself. In these pages, readers will find images of many items featured in the exhibit, along with additional rare treasures saved by Cline and her family, friends, and business associates. Likewise, both the book and the exhibit feature memories shared in interviews with those who knew and worked with this great singer.

To provide insight into Cline's many contributions to the music world, we invited Paul Kingsbury, a noted Cline expert and a widely published author in the field of country music, to prepare an in-depth essay on her career. A former museum staff member, Kingsbury annotated MCA's 1991 box set *The Patsy Cline Collection* and the label's 2003 multi-artist tribute album *Remembering Patsy Cline*. In addition, he has edited such landmark works as *The Encyclopedia of Country Music* (1998; 2012) and *Will the Circle Be Unbroken: Country Music in America* (2006).

Rosanne Cash, one of many genre-spanning performers who have drawn inspiration from Cline in the decades since her untimely death, offers a personal tribute to Cline, one of her musical heroes.

It is our hope that these essays and reminiscences—together with the images they accompany—provide a revealing picture of an extraordinary artist who rose to fame during a remarkable time of transition in America's musical and cultural history. Patsy Cline left an indelible mark that shows no sign of fading a half-century after her death.

—Mick Buck and John W. Rumble

Contributors

ROSANNE CASH joined singer-songwriters such as Rodney Crowell, Steve Earle, and Dwight Yoakam to give country music a youthful new edge in the 1980s. Among her eleven #1 singles are "Blue Moon with Heartache," "Seven Year Ache," and "I Don't Know Why You Don't Want Me," all of which she wrote. Her 1985 album *Rhythm & Romance* won a Grammy for Best Country Vocal Performance, Female. Cash has published *Bodies of Water*, a collection of short stories; a children's book; and a collection of short fiction by songwriters. In 2009 she released *The List*, an album based on a list of key country songs her father compiled for her when she was eighteen. The multi-talented Cash published *Composed*, a well-received memoir, in 2010.

PAUL KINGSBURY is a leading authority on the life and career of Patsy Cline. He compiled and annotated MCA's best-selling 1991 boxed set *The Patsy Cline Collection*, in addition to annotating the label's 2003 various-artists tribute album *Remembering Patsy Cline*. Along with his notes for many other albums and box sets, he is also the author of several books on country music, including *The Grand Ole Opry History of Country Music*. In addition, he is a coauthor of *Hatch Show Print: The History of a Great American Poster Shop*. Kingsbury edited *The Encyclopedia of Country Music, Country: The Music and the Musicians*, and *Will the Circle Be Unbroken: Country Music in America*, all landmarks of country music research. He served on the staff of the Country Music Hall of Fame® and Museum from 1985 through 2001, and is now communications director for The Nature Conservancy in Tennessee.

Gold lamé boots, worn by Patsy Cline.
Courtesy of the family of Patsy Cline / Photo by Bob Delevante

HONOR THY MUSIC®

August 24, 2012

Dear Museum Friend,

Almost fifty years after her untimely death on March 5, 1963, Patsy Cline is more popular than she was in her lifetime. Entirely self-possessed and fully aware of her vocal gifts, Patsy was confident and free well before feminism became a national movement.

Born in poverty and the child of a broken home, Patsy struggled long and hard before she found believers like Ott Devine, who recruited her for the Grand Ole Opry, and Owen Bradley, who helped her make the records that not only secured her fame and fortune, but redefined country music in the wake of rock & roll. In 1973, Patsy became the first female solo artist to be inducted into the Country Music Hall of Fame. Women in popular music still measure their vocal prowess against her supranatural contralto.

It is our great privilege to be entrusted with the safekeeping of Patsy's remarkable music and story. Since the opening of our museum in 1967, we have archived her recordings and preserved magazines, photos, and business files that document her remarkable career. In 1991, MCA released a comprehensive four-CD box set produced by the museum and showcasing Patsy's entire Decca catalog, the best of her 4 Star tracks, and radio transcriptions and live performances, including ten previously unreleased recordings.

In 2000, we offered *Love Always, Patsy: Letters from the Jewelry Box*, an exhibit featuring letters handwritten by Patsy to Treva Miller Steinbicker, an appreciative early follower who established Patsy's fan club and became her friend and confidante. Through Patsy's own words, we learned about the values, determination, and struggles that fueled her musical luminescence.

The exhibit *Patsy Cline: Crazy for Loving You*, like this accompanying book, builds upon those earlier efforts. The exhibit will remain open until June 2013. Along the way, there will be many related live performances, panels, films, and other programs enhanced by records, film and video clips, and other items from our collection. Some of these events will be streamed live at www.countrymusichalloffame.org, where you can also find a schedule of all Museum programs. We'll enjoy welcoming you to the exhibit, and we hope you'll be crazy about Patsy, too.

Sincerely,

Kyle Young, Director
Country Music Hall of Fame® and Museum

Acknowledgments

This book and the exhibit it complements represent the contributions of many individuals and organizations. First, we are greatly indebted to Julie Fudge, Patsy Cline's daughter, and Charlie Dick, Cline's husband from 1957 until her death in 1963, for their cooperation and support. Items loaned by Ms. Fudge, Mr. Dick, and the family of Patsy Cline included Cline's handwritten autobiography dating from 1962; undated, handwritten notes about her figure; a sizable scrapbook, and a trove of important artifacts, photos, clippings, posters, and other materials. In addition, Mario Munoz made his own extensive collection of Cline-related treasures available to the Country Music Hall of Fame® and Museum. Greg Hall, of TH Entertainment, supplied valuable archival footage. Others who loaned important items include Guy Cesario, Bill Cox, Judy Sue Huyett-Kemf of Celebrating Patsy Cline, Wayne Lensing of Historic Auto Attractions, Philip Martin, the Patsy Cline Partnership, Theresa Shalaby, Jimmy Walker, and C. Mark Willix.

Special thanks go to Harold Bradley, Brenda Lee, Willie Nelson, and Ray Walker for sharing memories of Cline in videotaped interviews shown in the exhibit. Over the years, other individuals also contributed interviews about Cline to the Museum's archives; these include Sarah Cannon (Minnie Pearl), Hank Cochran, Charlie Dick, Roy Drusky, Ray Edenton, Ralph Emery, Durwood Haddock, Buddy Harman, George Hamilton IV, Don Helms, Harlan Howard, Jan Howard, Loretta Lynn, Roger Miller, Bob Moore, and Grant Turner.

Many museum staff members devoted time and talent to the exhibit and book alike. Space prohibits listing them all, but some deserve mentioning here. Vice President for Museum Services Carolyn Tate led the exhibit's curatorial team, consisting of principal curator Mick Buck; curators Tim Davis, Kelli Hix, and Alan Stoker; registrar Elek Horvath; and production manager Lee Rowe. Creative Director Warren Denney, lead designer Margaret Pesek, exhibition designer Emily Marlow, and designer Brandon Riesgo brought their skills to bear as well. Vice President for Museum Programs Jay Orr oversaw the work of principal writer and editor John Rumble and editor Michael McCall.

We would also like to thank the Great American Country Television Network (GAC), supporting sponsor of the exhibition, as well as the Metro Nashville Arts Commission and the Tennessee Arts Commission, both of which provide essential operating support that underwrites museum publications, school programs, and public programs.

Finally, we are deeply grateful to Rosanne Cash for her insightful essay, which embodies her longstanding dedication to the museum and its mission.

Earrings from Patsy Cline's personal collection.
Courtesy of the family of Patsy Cline / Photo by Bob Delevante

Contents

The Cline

BY ROSANNE CASH

Somewhere in the blackout of early childhood, I had an encounter with Patsy Cline.

My father came home off the road at the end of a tour in the early '60s, and he had a passel of musicians in tow. Patsy was among them. There was something dark and secret about her inclusion in the group, and about my father bringing her home: She was having some trouble with Charlie, her husband, or she was deeply exhausted from constant touring, or there was some unspoken crisis of indeterminate importance. My parents talked about her quietly, away from everyone else. I remember my mother's awe. My mother worshipped her. Patsy, in the height of her artistic and personal magnificence, lived out the unexpressed lives of many, many women of the '50s and early '60s.

Patsy was powerful, charismatic, sexy, and full-bodied in every way. You only had to hear her sing the first two lines of "Walkin' After Midnight" or "I Fall to Pieces" to know that.

She was exquisitely self-determined. If she had insecurities, they were not the loudest note in her personality. She didn't seem to have a need for approval, and she never pandered to an audience. She just stood and let go with that Voice and filled the room, awakened our hearts, and stoked our imaginations. As a performer, she was calm, focused, and unmistakably PATSY. Who else was like her? She was almost instantly iconic, from her first record, and when she died at the age of thirty, that icon status quickly expanded into legend. But she is something more: a true original, completely unique, and one of the most influential and recognizable singers of the twentieth century. The first female solo artist elected to the Country Music Hall of Fame, she was one of the first women in country music to headline her own show, and to receive top billing above the male artists.

She had a "mouth like a sailor," as my mother told me (with barely repressed admiration) and made herself one

Photo Courtesy of Mario Munoz

of the boys, sidling up to the bar to share a beer and a dirty joke, while at the same time encouraging other women singers, giving them advice, guidance, and even her own clothing. She wryly referred to herself at the height of her fame as "The Cline." We who followed, and we who longed for her kind of charisma and were inspired by her originality and independence, owe her a tremendous debt.

But behind all that power and artistic capacity and breathtaking vocal style was a girl who collected earrings and salt and pepper shakers, who longed for time alone after the rigors of touring and promotion, who worried about paying for two new tires for her brand new Oldsmobile, who designed the clothes her mother made for her, who worked herself to the point of distraction and exhaustion, and who confided to her fan club president about her husband Charlie: "Treva, I've never loved a man so much in my life. He is my life, my world, just my everything." She was utterly female in the way women put love and relationships at the center of their lives, no matter how many hit records they have. She also poignantly confided to Treva in 1956, "I have no luck anymore at just everyday living." Then she added, "As far as singing, everything is looking up." Was it ever. In 1957, barely two years after signing her first recording contract, she answered a query from Treva about record sales: "Well as far as I knew 2 weeks ago we had sold 600,000 and was still selling 40,000 a day. Decca said I had already become their No 1 seller over Jerry Lewis, The Platters and Bill Haley, which made me feel proud."

We all feel proud. We claim her as our own, no matter who we are or what we listen to. She is on virtually every list ever compiled of the world's greatest singers and ranks high on VH1's *The 100 Greatest Women in Rock and Roll* and is #1 on CMT's *40 Greatest Women of Country Music*. She was and will always be Patsy with the instantly recognizable voice, the full-bodied and complex woman, sometimes walkin' after midnight, sometimes a little crazy, one of the true, true greats: The Cline. ■

Rosanne Cash

Above: The Cash family, early 1960s.
Left to right: Vivian, Rosanne, Cindy, Johnny and Kathleen.
Courtesy of Rosanne Cash

Right: Rosanne Cash, c. 1962.
Courtesy of Rosanne Cash

Opposite: Souvenir program for touring show headlined by Johnny Cash, 1962.
Courtesy of Mario Munoz

Unvanquished

PATSY CLINE'S IMMORTAL VOICE

BY PAUL KINGSBURY

TODAY, TOMORROW, AND FOREVER: THE PATSY CLINE LEGACY

There are other female singers of her era who had more hits. But none of them has had a greater and more lasting impact in both country and pop music.

Patsy Cline recorded for just eight years and released only three albums in her lifetime. She never wrote a hit song. She never won a Grammy. She never starred in a film or her own TV series. During her career, she was not a household name outside of country music. Only twelve of her singles reached the charts while she was living. Just two of her singles hit #1 on the country charts—"I Fall to Pieces" and "She's Got You." She died in a 1963 plane crash at age thirty, never knowing whether her musical legacy would endure.

Fifty years after her death, she is arguably still the world's most admired female country singer. In the late 1950s and early 1960s, she effortlessly bridged country music and pop, becoming country's first great torch singer and one of pop music's favorites. She had credibility with the country audience: In 1973, she became the first female solo singer elected to the Country Music Hall of Fame. And she had pop appeal: All but one of her country hits also climbed the pop charts, four of them reaching the Top Twenty.

Today Patsy Cline is far more popular than during her early 1960s heyday. Every commercial recording she ever made is in print—in many cases on multiple packages. Her 1967

Patsy Cline's mother, Hilda Hensley, accepts Cline's induction into the Country Music Hall of Fame, *CMA Awards Show*, October 15, 1973.
Front row (left to right): Conway Twitty, Loretta Lynn, Hensley, Charlie McCoy, Lew DeWitt (Statler Brothers), and Chet Atkins, who was also elected to the Hall of Fame that year. Second row (left to right): Roy Clark, RCA producer Bob Ferguson, arranger Bill McElhiney, and Statler Brothers members Phil Balsley, Harold Reid, and Don Reid.
Back Row (left to right): Charlie Rich and songwriter Kenny O'Dell. Roy Acuff leaves podium at left.

Greatest Hits album has been certified for sales of 10 million; it was the best-selling album by a female country singer until Shania Twain came along in the mid-'90s. Patsy's life story inspired the hit Hollywood movie *Sweet Dreams* (1985), starring Jessica Lange, and the long-running stage musical *Always...Patsy Cline*. Her short life has been documented in detail in half a dozen biographical books.

Her signature recordings—"I Fall to Pieces," "Crazy," "Walkin' After Midnight"—have been heard in television commercials and covered by everyone from Garth Brooks and Reba McEntire to Natalie Cole and Elvis Costello. "Crazy" is the best-selling jukebox hit of all time and was named to the Grammy Hall of Fame for recordings in 1992. "I Fall to Pieces" was named to the Grammy Hall of Fame in 2001. Forty years

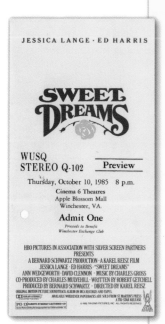

JESSICA LANGE · ED HARRIS

SWEET DREAMS

WUSQ
STEREO Q-102 | Preview

Thursday, October 10, 1985   8 p.m.

Cinema 6 Theatres
Apple Blossom Mall
Winchester, VA.

Admit One
*Proceeds to Benefit
Winchester Exchange Club*

HBO PICTURES IN ASSOCIATION WITH SILVER SCREEN PARTNERS
PRESENTS
A BERNARD SCHWARTZ PRODUCTION · A KAREL REISZ FILM
JESSICA LANGE · ED HARRIS "SWEET DREAMS"
ANN WEDGEWORTH · DAVID CLENNON · MUSIC BY CHARLES GROSS
CO-PRODUCED BY CHARLES MULDEHILL · WRITTEN BY ROBERT GETCHELL
PRODUCED BY BERNARD SCHWARTZ · DIRECTED BY KAREL REISZ
ORIGINAL MOTION PICTURE SOUNDTRACK ALBUM ON MCA RECORDS AND TAPES.
AVAILABLE WHEREVER PAPERBACKS ARE SOLD FROM ST. MARTIN'S PRESS
A TRI-STAR RELEASE

JESSICA LANGE · ED HARRIS

She fought harder, loved more and went further
than most people ever dream of.
Before there was a Coal Miner's Daughter there was Patsy Cline,
the one who inspired them all.
This is her true life and love story.

SWEET DREAMS

Above and right:
Preview ticket and
promotional flyer for the
1985 movie *Sweet Dreams*.
Courtesy of Julie Fudge

Far right: Costume worn
by Jessica Lange in
Sweet Dreams.
Photo by Bob Delevante

after her death, a 2002 Country Music Television poll of music insiders named

Patsy Cline the greatest of *40 Greatest Women of Country Music*.

But beyond all the honors, sales figures, and chart statistics, there is the

undeniable appeal of Patsy Cline herself—as a brilliant singer, as a role model

for women in the music business, and as a compelling story of personal tragedy

and artistic triumph.

First, there is her voice—a rich, powerful, natural wonder capable of vaulting

octaves with ease. A technically gifted singer, she routinely recorded rangy

tunes like "I Fall to Pieces" or "Sweet Dreams" in a single live take as the full studio band played beside her, with no overdubs to correct missed notes on her part. Though she could unleash an arsenal of vocal catches, slides, sobs, and growls, her touch was generally nuanced, with a full command of subtle emotional shadings. Added to these physical gifts was her ability to pour herself wholeheartedly into her songs, especially heartache songs such as "Crazy," "She's Got You," "Faded Love," and "Leavin' on Your Mind." Indeed, she made all her songs her own, her expressive voice welling up with tearful emotion or teasing with playful humor, depending on the song's mood.

"She absolutely felt the lyrics of her songs," said veteran Nashville studio guitarist Harold Bradley, who played on most of her sessions. "She put her heart and soul in all of those songs. People that have hit records are storytellers.... Patsy could really make you believe it happened."

"I sing just like I hurt inside" is the way Patsy described her style to Trudy Stamper, publicist for WSM radio in Nashville.

Patsy's songwriter friend Hank Cochran, who wrote several songs for her, put it this way in 2001: "I ain't heard nobody out-sing her yet, and I've been here forty-two years."

Above left: Cover of *Playbill*, the magazine of New York's Off-Broadway Variety Arts Theater, 1997.
Courtesy of Julie Fudge

Left: Cover for the LP *Patsy Cline's Greatest Hits* (1967), which has sold more than 10 million copies.

STOP, LOOK, AND LISTEN: PATSY CLINE'S VOCAL STYLE

Few singers are born with vocal gifts as prodigious as Patsy Cline's. Her voice was a beautiful instrument—a smooth, warm, flexible contralto that could easily span more than two octaves. Most of us have difficulty singing beyond a single octave. Listen to her 1960 studio recording of "Lovesick Blues." She ranges from the E below middle C up more than two octaves to end on a bell-like A4. She was not only blessed with a natural talent, she developed it. By the time she began recording in 1955, she had been singing professionally for nine years, starting at age fourteen. She had worked with country bands in bars and pop orchestras in supper clubs. She had learned how to wring convincing emotion out of a song—country or pop—and to project her voice enough to be heard over a crowd.

"She'd sing in all those clubs where she had to sing loud to be heard," said Gordon Stoker of the Jordanaires vocal backing group, who worked with her on sessions from 1959 to 1963. "And I think that's the reason she developed her lungs to belt it out, so to speak. Patsy sang louder in the studio on a microphone than most girls I remember we were recording with."

"It's a big voice," said Trisha Yearwood, a singer blessed with a powerful voice herself. "It's not a wimpy voice. It's not thin—ever. It's just big. The other thing about it is that it is very emotional. You hear the breath. It's like she's standing in the room with you, singing."

Though she never had formal singing lessons, Patsy Cline studied other singers on recordings and learned techniques

Patsy Cline recording in Owen Bradley's Nashville studio.
Photo by Elmer Williams

that would elevate her artistry beyond the norm. She followed pop singers as well as country ones. Her widower, Charlie Dick, remembers Kay Starr, Teresa Brewer, and Patti Page—all pop contemporaries of Patsy—were particular favorites of hers. "She had records, when I met her, of just about everybody in the business—female singers," said Dick.

"Patsy was a big fan of Kay Starr, and just listening to her sing you could tell she'd probably heard every record Kay Starr ever made," wrote Jimmy Dean in his autobiography. A brassy-

Continued on page 20

Songwriter's Friend

Patsy Cline was a favorite among Nashville's small but growing songwriting community, and her hits helped writers establish their own reputations. "She liked to laugh and have a good time," Hank Cochran remembered. "If you wanted her opinion on something and you asked her, you'd damn sure get it. She'd say, 'Hey, hoss. That ain't worth a damn.'... I'd say, 'Well, damn, Patsy. I like that song!' And she'd say, 'Why, hell. That ain't worth a damn, hoss.'"

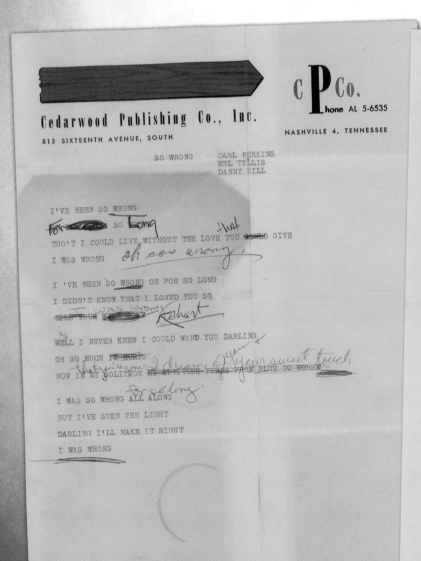

I Fall To Pieces

I fall to pieces each time I see you again
I fall to pieces. how can I be just your friend
You want me to ~~act~~ kissed like we've never kissed
You want me to forget
Pretend we've never met
And I've tried & I've tried but I haven't yet
You walk by and I fall to pieces

I fall to pieces each time some one speaks your name
I fall to pieces, time only adds to the flame
They tell me to find some one else to love
Some one who'll love me to
The way you use to do
But each time I go out with some one new, You walk by & I fall to pieces

Harlan Howard

"I do know that she loved to hang out with songwriters. She would come over, after her Opry song, she would come over to Tootsie's, and it wasn't necessarily looking for me, but looking for us, which would be Willie and Hank and I and Roger Miller, Mel Tillis, Wayne Walker, Justin Tubb, all of us guys. We were all buddies. Of course, she'd do anybody's song, but we had an inside track 'cause we were here."

Country Music Hall of Fame member Harlan Howard wrote several of Cline's hits.

Above: Patsy Cline's handwritten lyrics to "I Fall to Pieces," her 1961 hit written by Hank Cochran and Harlan Howard.
Courtesy of the family of Patsy Cline

Opposite, far left: Patsy's recording of Danny Dill, Carl Perkins, and Mel Tillis's "So Wrong" peaked at #14 on *Billboard*'s country chart in 1962.
Courtesy of the family of Patsy Cline

Opposite, left: Below Hank Cochran's lyrics to "Long, Slow Hurt," Patsy Cline wrote partial lyrics to Bob Montgomery's "Back in Baby's Arms." Her recording was released in 1963 as the B-side to "Sweet Dreams."
Courtesy of the family of Patsy Cline

Harlan Howard, c. 1961.

At the Mint Theater in Las Vegas, 1962. Left to right: Tompall Glaser, Joey Lemmon, Cline, unidentified drummer and bass player.

sounding high soprano, Starr logged more than thirty pop hits between 1948 and 1962. Most likely Patsy admired Kay Starr's skill with rhythm, word emphasis, and her emotional, full-throated intensity.

Patsy was also a lifelong country fan. Charlie Dick has mentioned smooth-singing Redd Stewart, Pee Wee King's vocalist, and big-voiced honky-tonker Ray Price as favorites of hers. She was a big fan of Elvis Presley, and she had a large color photo of him pasted to the back of her personal scrapbook. In addition, she collected records by Kitty Wells, Goldie Hill, Charline Arthur, Wanda Jackson, and other female country singers of the day.

Aside from her voice, part of what makes Patsy Cline's music so alluring is the tension between her genuine love of country music and the full, smooth, pop sound of her voice. Patsy recognized her innate pop ability, although she sometimes struggled with it because of her identification with country music and her rural upbringing. Nevertheless, she was also an ambitious woman who loved to sing to adoring crowds. She may not have thought of herself as a pop singer, but she was eventually willing to wear full-length, sequined evening gowns and sing in front of string sections if it would make her a star. However, it took some time for her to grow comfortable with making concessions to pop stardom.

Studying her contemporaries, Patsy picked up various vocal tricks: sobs; vocal throbs, catches, and hiccups; slides up to notes and down from them; half-yodels; growls; groans; vibrato; and exquisite breath control. In the first years of her recording career (1955–60), she occasionally leaned too heavily on these devices, not always heeding a song's lyrical message. That may have been her way of compensating for lackluster song material. However, between 1960 and 1963, she increasingly developed a tasteful sense of restraint in her technique. Throughout her studio years, her use of melisma (stretching a syllable into several notes) and vibrato were always sparing and carefully chosen for maximum impact. Instead of trying to impress us with her gift—as too many twenty-first-century pop and R&B singers do—Patsy Cline focused on inhabiting each song as an actress would a role and telling its story unforgettably.

She was the consummate professional: a confident, commanding vocalist. She may have worried early on about landing hit records, but she never doubted her vocal abilities. "Patsy liked to sing and she was a good singer, and she knew she was a good singer," recalled Jimmy Dean, who fronted the Washington, D.C.–area TV show *Town & Country Time*, where Patsy gained early exposure.

"I remember the musicians used to tell me the difference [between] Patsy and other people recording was that she drove the band," said radio and TV host Ralph Emery. "The band would dominate other people—the recording band—and would drive the singer. But Patsy came in and sang with such gusto that she drove the band. And they loved to work with her."

Continued on page 23

Billboard ad, December 8, 1962. *Courtesy of Mario Munoz*

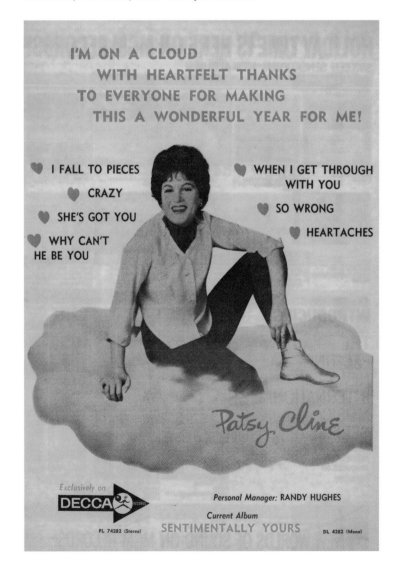

Charlie Dick
PATSY'S MUSICAL TASTES

"When Patsy and I started going together, a record would come on the radio and she'd say who it was, and she knew something about every record on the radio. And half the guys I hadn't heard of....

"She liked Kay Starr. She had records, when I met her, of just about everybody in the business—female singers. Kay Starr and Teresa Brewer. She even had Sophie Tucker records. She had Goldie Hill records; she had Wanda Jackson records; she had Charline Arthur records. Kitty Wells....

"One guy she said she liked his singing very much was Redd Stewart, who was with Pee Wee King. And of course we both liked Ray Price. She liked western swing music real well....

"I remember she bought an album one time. It was the soundtrack to a movie. Gogi Grant was singing on it—*The Helen Morgan Story*. And I don't recall now whether she really got into Helen Morgan or got into Gogi Grant. But I know that album was played many times in our house."

Charlie Dick was married to Patsy Cline
from 1957 until her untimely death.

Charlie Dick's ID bracelet, with flip-top compartment containing photos of Patsy Cline, was a gift from Cline to her husband.
Courtesy of Charlie Dick / Photo by Bob Delevante

COME ON IN (AND MAKE YOURSELF AT HOME): THE REAL PATSY CLINE

What was Patsy Cline like as a person? She had brown wavy hair and brown eyes. She stood 5 feet 5½ inches tall, and generally weighed around 135 pounds. In her prime she had a nice figure, measuring 36–25¾–38, according to handwritten notes she left.

"I think her wardrobe had a lot to do with the fact that she was known as a sex symbol," recalled the late Sarah Cannon, better known as Minnie Pearl. "She wore tight clothes. Tight around her hips.... She had a full figure. She was not overweight."

Patsy collected earrings, salt and pepper shakers, and photos of country music stars. She liked to cook southern-style dishes and keep her house looking nice. She was the wife of printing press operator Charlie Dick (married September 15, 1957) and a devoted, doting mother to two young children, Julie and Randy, who were just four-and-a-half and two years old when she died.

Far left: Newlyweds, Mountain Side Inn, Winchester, Virginia, September 15, 1957.
Courtesy of Julie Fudge and Charlie Dick

Left: Patsy Cline's engraved silver ring.
Courtesy of Charlie Dick
Photo by Bob Delevante

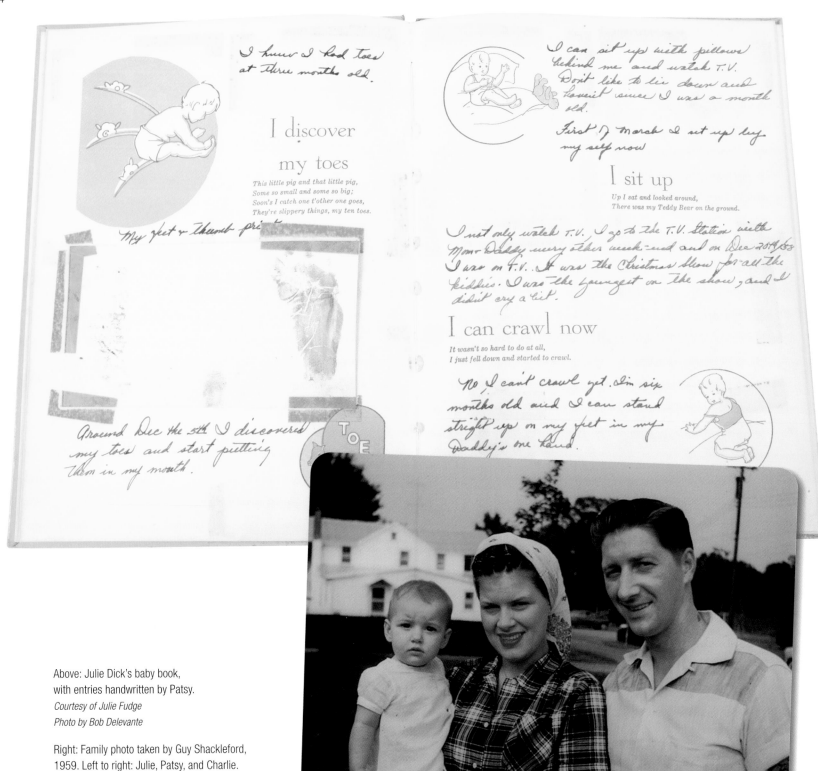

Above: Julie Dick's baby book,
with entries handwritten by Patsy.
Courtesy of Julie Fudge
Photo by Bob Delevante

Right: Family photo taken by Guy Shackleford,
1959. Left to right: Julie, Patsy, and Charlie.
Courtesy of Julie Fudge and Charlie Dick

Virtually everyone she knew in the Nashville music business liked her. She could be brassy and bull-headed and would often curse with abandon, but she was also a soft touch for a person in need and had a warm, maternal streak a mile wide. She tended to call people she liked "hoss" and sometimes referred to herself humorously as "The Cline." To her husband Charlie and her closest friends, she was "Pat." She was lusty, fun-loving, and full of life.

"She just wanted to be a 'good old back-slappin' one of the boys' kind of girl," Jimmy Dean wrote in his autobiography. "It's true she would cuss like a sailor, especially when she was mad, but she could also be warm and sweet."

Continued on page 28

Above, left to right: Patsy, Julie, Randy, and Charlie Dick, c. 1962.

Right: Letter written by Patsy Cline to her mother-in-law, Mary Dick, dated May 30, 1960.
Courtesy of the family of Patsy Cline

Nashville Tenn.
May 30/60

Dear Mary:

Suppose you are thinking we have forgotten how to write but I just got back home last Wed. and had Big Betty & Little Betty here when I arrived. Then after riding 1750 miles home had 2 washings to do and of course the cooking I had to do for all. Then last Fri & Sat I had to go to Chattnooga Tenn. to do a T.V. spot and do the Opry on Sat nite. They left Sun. then Hank Mills a song writer from up home came in to stay a week and he's leaving today. So Sat. nite this past I had the Opry to do and after the Opry we left & went to Chattanooga again to do a park date there yesterday. So you can see why I havn't had much time. I called Mom the night you were operated ... address and I'll send them a card sometime.

Well I guess I'll close and get to work. Charlie goes to work in about an hour. Tell Melvin "hello" for us and we wish he could spend some time with us this summer, but I know you will need him when you get home.

We will be wondering how you are & when you go home from the hospital, so let us know.

Tell all "hello". Love always,
Pat, Julie & Charlie

Loretta Lynn

"MUSIC IN THE WIND"

"Patsy was really the best girlfriend I had in Nashville, Tennessee, in the music business. Patsy done so much for me. The night that she was killed, we were going to go to the [store] the next day, and she was going to buy me a rug for my house. She'd already made drapes for my house. I didn't have any furniture in my front room or anything, but she was going to buy me a rug and then buy me a piece of furniture at a time.

"That night I went to bed, and I thought, 'I won't turn on the radio, because we're going to get up early.' I remember laying and listening to the wind blow. As a little girl, I remember when the wind blew, things would happen.... It sounded like there was music in the wind. I knew something was going to happen, but I didn't know what. I never dreamed it would be about Patsy."

Country Music Hall of Fame member Loretta Lynn
joined the Grand Ole Opry cast in 1962.

Patsy Cline's jewelry box and earrings, from her personal collection.
Courtesy of the family of Patsy Cline
Photos by Bob Delevante

"Patsy thought nothing of going to the supermarket and buying a couple of bagfuls of groceries and dropping them off to someone who needed them," the late Dottie West told Cline biographer Ellis Nassour. "If there were kids involved, she was especially thoughtful. And she was constantly giving away clothes. And money!"

Patsy Cline struggled for years to succeed in an era when women were not only afterthoughts in country music but also second-class citizens in American life in general. The word *feminism* was then unknown in America. Because she made her own way in an industry run by men, where women singers were often looked upon as uncommercial

and sometimes even unnecessary, she took special care to nurture and help other female singers. Loretta Lynn, Dottie West, Jan Howard, and even teenagers Brenda Lee and Barbara Mandrell all have remarked on how much Patsy looked out for them and supported them in their own careers.

"The women singers did not have the clout they have today," West told Ellis Nassour in an interview he later adapted into the foreword to his biography. "And, more than anyone, Patsy opened the door for us. She made the producers and record labels believe we could sell records, and the promoters see that we could draw audiences rather than merely being the fill-in presence we had become.

"Patsy was bright and intelligent. No one would think of her as dumb. Oh, no! If they did, they'd sure as hell soon find out! Patsy made the men singers and promoters respect her and the success she achieved. Some of us are feminine and soft, and Patsy had those qualities, but she could also hold her own against any man."

Continued on page 32

Dottie West and Patsy Cline, c. 1961.
Courtesy of Julie Fudge and Charlie Dick

Salt and pepper shaker sets from Patsy Cline's personal collection.
Courtesy of the family of Patsy Cline / Photos by Bob Delevante

Ginny Hensley (Patsy Cline) on stage in Winchester, Virginia, c. 1948. Left to right: Ken Windle, MC Jack Fretwell, Frank Patton, Hensley, Virginia Taylor, Benny Brown, unidentified.
Courtesy of Julie Fudge and Charlie Dick

WHO CAN I COUNT ON: PATSY CLINE'S BEGINNINGS

She could make you believe her stories of heartache because she had lived them, packing a lifetime of love and disappointment and struggle into just thirty years. Patsy Cline accomplished much, but it was an uphill battle all the way.

She was born Virginia Patterson Hensley in the sleepy Shenandoah Valley town of Winchester, Virginia, six days after her parents married. Her father, Sam Hensley, the proud scion of a rich family fallen on hard times, was forty-three;

her mother, Hilda Virginia Patterson, was a sixteen-year-old farmer's daughter. It was a bad match from the start, destined for failure.

Almost from birth, Patsy (known then as Ginny) was a show-off, always trying to catch her father's fleeting attention. By the age of four she had won a local tap-dancing contest. Her father and mother both sang in church (Pentecostal

Continued on page 34

Jan Howard

PATSY'S SERIOUS SIDE

"We were opposite, in a lot of ways. I was real quiet, I guess backwards, you might say, and Patsy was so outgoing. But she had a very serious side about her that a lot of people didn't see. I didn't see it real often, you know, but she came over to the house one time, after she was pregnant with Randy, her little boy. She came over, and she was down in the dumps. She had to go somewhere to work. Things just weren't working out right. She was struggling. We talked about—just serious girl talk. It was serious, woman-to-woman talk, and friend-to-friend.... But I think she tried to hide that a lot, by the big, booming laugh and all this and that. I have no documentation on that, but I saw behind the scenes, and I saw behind the smiles, sometimes. But when she was happy, she was really happy. She loved her children, loved her children very much....

"We never talked about religion.... But some of the songs she sang, I think she would have to be a spiritual person, or she couldn't have sung them like she did. We were sitting over at her house one day, and we were singing back and forth, just sitting there with a guitar. And we were singing duet on "Just as I Am," and "Just a Closer Walk with Thee."... I have a feeling when someone sings an inspirational or religious song whether they really know what they're singing about. And I think Patsy did."

Jan Howard met Patsy Cline while guesting on the Grand Ole Opry in 1960. Howard joined the cast in 1971.

and Baptist) and liked music, and her musical talent blossomed quickly. String band leader Walter Smith said that at the age of seven Patsy performed with his troupe in 1939. With encouragement from an older half-sister, Patsy learned to play piano by ear, starting at age eight, when on her birthday she received the piano she'd been begging for. She listened regularly to the radio, and her favorite program was the Saturday night broadcast of the Grand Ole Opry from Nashville station WSM. "From the time she was about ten," Hilda Hensley told biographer Ellis Nassour, "Patsy was living, eating, and sleeping country music. I know she never wanted anything so badly as to be a star on the Grand Ole Opry."

By age fourteen, she had managed to gain a regular spot singing on local country station WINC. But even if she sang her heart out, she couldn't hold on to her father, who was reportedly often drunk and angry. In later years, Patsy hinted strongly that he had made sexual advances on her. He left the family shortly after she turned fifteen. To make ends meet, Patsy's mother became a seamstress, and Patsy quit high school to work in a local drugstore. Absolutely determined to make it as a singer, Patsy made time for music whenever she could.

"On Saturdays," she recalled years later, "I worked all day in Hunter Gaunt's drugstore in Winchester, and then at night, my mother drove me to Front Royal, where I sang pop tunes in a supper club from 10 p.m. to 1 a.m. We wouldn't get home and in bed until about three o'clock in the morning. A few hours later I was up, getting ready to return to work in the drugstore."

One of Patsy Cline's stage costumes,
designed by Patsy and created by her mother, Hilda, c. 1956.
Photo by Bob Delevante

With members of the Kountry Krackers and others, Newton D. Baker Veteran's Hospital, Martinsburg, West Virginia, 1955.
Left to right: Joseph B. Luttrell, Dave Hawthorne, Wilbur Sellers, Ralph Lamp, Patsy Cline, Johnny Anderson, and Raleigh Easter.
Courtesy of Julie Fudge and Charlie Dick

Early on, she often sang in the area with Ralph "Jumbo" Rinker, a local pop music pianist. Rinker played regional lounges, and with him she sang pop numbers like "Smoke Gets in Your Eyes," "Stormy Weather," and "I Only Have Eyes for You." In time, she also began singing with the Jack Fretwell Orchestra at a local nightclub called the Yorks Inn. Fretwell's group was a small-town big band, and like most big bands during the late 1940s they played pop songs. As a result, Patsy regularly performed material such as

"Embraceable You," "Stardust," and "You Made Me Love You," which Judy Garland had immortalized in 1937. Patsy was laying the groundwork for the smooth vocal style that would characterize her biggest hits.

Yet she still had her heart set on being a country singer at the Grand Ole Opry. By 1948 or '49, she managed through sheer chutzpah and the intercession of Grand Ole Opry performer Wally Fowler to land an audition with Opry manager Jim Denny, despite the fact that she was still not

Scraps

legally old enough to join. It would take more than a decade of hard work before she returned to Nashville and the Opry to stay.

In addition to high-toned supper club engagements, Patsy continued to sing country music at local nightclubs, VFWs, and the Moose Lodge in Brunswick, Maryland, invariably wearing the flashy, fringed cowgirl outfits Patsy herself designed and her mother sewed for her. At age twenty, she met local country bandleader Bill Peer, who became her de facto manager and persuaded her to change her name from Ginny to Patsy. In 1953, she married Gerald Cline, and her stage name was complete (though the marriage would end in 1957). Through Peer's efforts, she began to climb towards real success. She recorded her first demo. She won first prize at the August 1954 National Championship Country Music Contest in Warrenton, Virginia. Subsequently, she was selected to appear regularly on *Town & Country Time*, a Washington, D.C., regional TV broadcast produced by local impresario Connie B. Gay. That fall, at age twenty-two, she signed a recording contract. It appeared she was on her way.

Continued on page 40

Opposite: A scrapbook Cline entrusted to Dottie West. This book was later damaged in a fire at West's home. *Courtesy of the family of Patsy Cline / Photo by Bob Delevante*

Left: With George Hamilton IV, backstage at Connie B. Gay's *Town & Country Jamboree*, Washington, D.C., 1956.

Costume Design

PATSY'S PERSONAL STYLE

Patsy Cline designed many of her own dresses, sketching the shape and details for her mother, who brought the designs to life. These are some of Patsy's drawings and notations.

Courtesy of the family of Patsy Cline

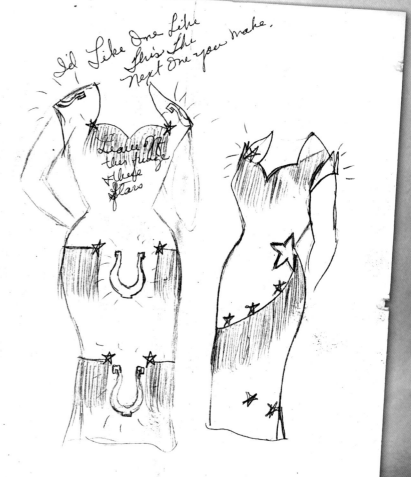

Minnie Pearl

"I think her wardrobe had a lot to do with her being known as a sex symbol. She wore tight clothes. Tight around her hips. Flashy material. She went in for sequins and lamé, gold and silver lamé. And she went in for a little shorter dresses than most of those girls were wearing at that point. Patsy stuck to shirtwaist-type dresses, but very tight. And she could wear 'em. She knew how to wear 'em. And high-heeled shoes. It kind of went with her. I mean, it was the package. She had a full figure; she was not overweight. I just think she was a big girl. She was a sexy girl. I would like to see her walk out and compete with some of these girls now. I've seen some television stuff that they've unearthed. It doesn't begin to do her justice."

Country Music Hall of Fame member Minnie Pearl
(Sarah Cannon; 1912–96) was a Grand Ole Opry star from 1940 to 1991.

MOVING ALONG: THE EVOLUTION OF HER SOUND

Patsy Cline had many unlucky breaks in her career. One lucky one was the record producer and arranger selected for her: Owen Bradley. A Nashville pop orchestra leader and former staff pianist and music director for Nashville's WSM radio, by 1947 he was assisting Decca Records' country A&R (artist and repertoire) man Paul Cohen on his Nashville sessions. Bradley quickly became Cohen's right-hand man on the local scene, lining up musicians for recording sessions and then arranging the music for the New York–based executive, who was not a musician. With encouragement from Cohen, Bradley opened a series of his own recording studios in Nashville starting in 1952. Around Christmas of

1954, Bradley moved his studio operations into a fifty-year-old clapboard, foursquare house at 804 Sixteenth Avenue South in a run-down neighborhood. He called the facility Bradley Film and Recording Studios and opened it for business in April 1955. It was the first recording studio on what would someday become known as Music Row.

When Patsy Cline came to Bradley, she was not signed to Decca Records. She was instead signed to a small, independent California label known as 4 Star Records, which leased her recordings to Decca. The agreement allowed Decca's Cohen to choose the recording site and producer. The smaller label was owned by Bill McCall, who had earned his fortune operating mines for copper and fluorspar (an ingredient in shellac records) before buying a controlling stake in 4 Star in the late 1940s.

McCall had a well-deserved reputation for cheating recording artists and his in-house stable of songwriters out of their royalties. Patsy Cline knew none of this when the twenty-two-year-old signed with McCall on September 30, 1954. She agreed to a meager royalty of 2.34 percent of retail price—less than half what country singers on major record labels like Decca and RCA were earning. She never received a penny in royalties during her five-year stint with 4 Star Records, though she was paid a few thousand dollars

PATSY CLINE

4 STAR SALES - BMI
PC-EPF-12

promotional
record
NOT FOR SALE

Autographed promotional record issued by 4 Star Sales,
Bill McCall's music publishing firm, c. 1955.
Courtesy of Theresa Shalaby

Recording contract and royalty statement from 4 Star Record Company.
Courtesy of Charlie Dick and the family of Patsy Cline

4 STAR RECORD COMPANY INC.

305 SOUTH FAIR OAKS AVENUE
PASADENA 1, CALIFORNIA

July 1, 1960

Miss Patsy Cline,
213 E. Marthona Rd.,
Madison, Tennessee.

Dear Miss Cline:

Enclosed please find Royalty statement for the period Jan. 1 to June 30, 1960 inc.

Yours very truly,

FOUR STAR RECORD CO. INC.,

by *Wm. A. McCall*
Wm. A. McCall, President

WAMC:gw
encl:3

Date September 30, 1954

PATSY CLINE
Name of Artist

824-A East Patrick St,
Address

Frederick, MD.

Dear Patsy Cline:

1. This contract for the personal services of musicians is made between Four Star Record Co. Inc., as the employer and you and the musicians who, from time to time during the term of this agreement, make up the orchestra represented by you as leader.

2. We hereby employ the personal services of you and such musicians individually, and you and such musicians will perform together for us under your leadership for the purpose of making phonograph records.

3. Recordings will be made at recording sessions, in our studios, at mutually agreeable times during the term hereof. A minimum of 16 78 r.p.m. record sides, or the equivalent thereof, shall be recorded during the period of this contract, and additional recordings shall be made at our election. The musical compositions to be recorded shall be mutually agreed upon between you and us, and each recording shall be subject to our approval as satisfactory, for manufacture and sale. As to each recording session a separate Form B contract, on the form then approved by the American Federation of Musicians of the United States and Canada (hereinafter called the "Federation") shall be entered into. No recording shall be made by dubbing.

4. We will pay you in respect of recordings made hereunder, a royalty of 2.34 % of the retail list price in the country of manufacture, of 90% of all records sold embodying performances hereunder on both sides thereof, and one-half the amount of such royalty for 90% of all records sold embodying performances hereunder on only one side thereof; provided, however, that for records sold in Europe we may, from time to time, at our election, base the percentages either upon the retail list prices in the country of manufacture, or the retail list prices in England. Royalties for records sold outside of the United States are to be computed in the national currency of the country where the retail list prices above mentioned apply, and are to be payable only when such royalties are received by us in the United States and in the dollar equivalent at the rate of exchange at the time we receive payment.

5. For the services of the musicians hereunder, we will make a non-returnable payment to the musicians within fourteen days after the services are rendered, or earlier, if demanded by any local of the American Federation of Musicians in whose jurisdiction the recording engagement takes place, at the rate of $ scale for each record side or at the rate of union scale, whichever is greater; and such payments shall be charged against your royalties when earned. We will render an accounting to you within forty-five days after June 30th and after December 31st of each year during which records made hereunder are sold.

6. During the period of this contract you will not perform for the purpose of making phonograph records for any person other than us. After the expiration of this contract you will not perform any musical composition recorded hereunder for any other person for the purpose of making phonograph records, within five years after our recording is made. You acknowledge that your services are unique and extraordinary.

7. All recordings and all records and reproductions made therefrom, together with the performances embodied therein, shall be entirely our property, free of any claims whatsoever by you or any person deriving any rights or interests from you. Without limitation of the foregoing, we shall have the right to make records or other reproductions of the performances embodied in such recordings by any method now or hereafter known, and to sell and deal in the same under any trade marks or trade names or labels designated by us, or we may at our election refrain therefrom. Nothing herein contained shall deprive the musicians of any rights which may hereafter be created in their favor in or in connection with the use in public performances of recordings made hereunder.

---

14. The period of this contract shall be two year(s) commencing with the date hereof.

15. The Federation will not approve any such agreement unless provision is made for the recording of at least eight (8) sides during each year of the term of the agreement.

16. The term of any agreement, including all options, cannot exceed three (3) years.

You grant us the option to renew this contract for a period of one year(s) upon all the terms and conditions herein contained, except for the option to renew for a further period. This option may be exercised by us by giving you notice in writing at least thirty days prior to the expiration hereof; and such notice to you may be given by delivery to you personally or by mailing to you at your address last known to us.

Very truly yours,

FOUR STAR RECORD COMPANY Inc.,

By *Wm. A. McCall* Pres
Employer

ACCEPTED

x *Patsy Cline*
Leader and Representatives of Employees

Bill Peer
WITNESS:

Charles Town, W.Va.
Address:

ROYALTY STATEMENT OF (Page 1)

PATSY CLINE

FOR THE PERIOD Jan. 1 to June 30, 1960

RELEASE NO.	QUANTITY	RATE	AMOUNT
MASTERS LEASED BY CORAL:			
Honkey Tonk Merry-Go-Round	139	.01	$1.39
Turn The Cards Slowly	139	.01	1.39
MASTERS LEASED BY DECCA:			
That Wonderful Someone	98	.01	.98
Hungry For Love	98	.01	.98
That Wonderful Someone	228	.04	9.12
I Can't Forget	228	.04	9.12
A Poor Man's Roses	532	.01	5.32
Walking After Midnight	532	.01	5.32
Today, Tomorrow & Forever	164	.01	1.64
Try Again	164	.01	1.64
Three Cigarettes In An Ask Tray	185	.01	1.85
A Stranger In My Arms	185	.01	1.85
Stop The World	153	.01	1.53
Walking Dream	153	.01	1.53
Dear God	92	.01	.92
He Will Do For You	92	.01	.92
You Understand	2026	.01	20.26
Gotta Lot of Rhythm	4024	.01	40.24
I'm Blue Again	4024	.01	40.24
CANADA			
Stop The World			
Walking Dream	25	.022	.55
Come On In			
Let The Teardrops Fall	28	.022	.61
I Can See An Angel			
Never No More	45	.022	.99
If I Could See The World Thru The Eyes Of A Child			
Just Out Of Reach Of My Two Open Arms	153	.022	3.37
Stop The World			
Walking Dream	29	.02	.58
Come On In			
Let The Teardrops Fall	42	.02	.84
I Can See An Angel			
Never No More	135	.02	2.70

FOUR STAR RECORD COMPANY INC.

BY: *Wm. A. McCall*

in advances on royalties. Perhaps worse, her 4 Star contract gave McCall the right to approve the material she recorded. For his part, McCall was mostly interested in using the label to earn songwriting and publishing royalties by getting his 4 Star artists to record only songs that he published (and often took composer credit on). He also gained revenue by leasing his recordings to major labels for distribution. That is how Patsy Cline's recordings—though made for 4 Star—were released on the Decca label and its subsidiary Coral during the late 1950s.

Fortunately for Patsy, Decca country recording chief Paul Cohen saw potential in her and enlisted the gifted Owen Bradley to help him produce her records. Bradley recognized immediately that Patsy Cline had an unusually accomplished, pop-friendly voice. But he was concerned about taking that voice in a blatantly pop direction, lest he displease Decca's top brass in New York. "Well, in the beginning we were trying to be country like Jean Shepard and Kitty Wells," he told journalist Bob Millard. "If we'd have made Patsy Cline in the '50s like we did in the '60s, we wouldn't have survived in the '50s. They would have said, 'What are you sending us those Kay Starr records or those pop records for?' See, they would have been so much like pop records. They would have said, 'You're the country department. If you're going to make pop records either come up here or you're fired.'"

From 1955 through 1960, Cline and Bradley searched for a winning formula, trying hard-core country weepers, hillbilly swing tunes, rockabilly boppers, cocktail lounge ballads, even

Continued on page 46

Above: Sitting pretty, mid-1950s.

Opposite: Cover of the Washington, D.C., *Sunday Star*, March 18, 1956.
Courtesy of Mario Munoz

HILLBILLY WITH OOMPH: PATSY CLINE . . . pages 2 and 11

STAR COLOR PHOTO BY ELWOOD BAKER

Patsy and Her Fans

In 1955, Patsy Cline began corresponding with Treva Miller, a young woman from Telford, Tennessee, who organized Patsy's first fan club and ran it until her own untimely death in an automobile accident in 1959. Through her fan club journal, Miller helped Cline communicate with those whose love and attention the singer valued so highly.

"Treva," Patsy wrote not long after winning the *Arthur Godfrey's Talent Scouts* contest in 1957, "thank all these wonderful people for me that are writing to me. I just can't get the time out to write each one of them. I just never received such letters in my life. I just sit right down and cry every time I get a pile of them."

Above: With Treva Miller, c. 1956. *Courtesy of Mario Munoz*

Below: One of the first of many letters from Patsy Cline to Treva Miller.

Questions

Q. When and where were you born?
A. In Winchester, Va, Sept 8th 1932

Q. How long have you been singing?
A. 16 years. But Professionally 9. years.

Q. Who gave you your first break?
A. Wally Fowler made it possible for me to sing at N.B.M.

Q. What Musical instruments do you play?
A. Piano.

Q. What is your all time favorite song?
A. Satisfied Mind. or Just A Closer Walk With Thee.

Q. What was the biggest thrill to you in your career?
A. When I sang on the Grande Ole Opry. In July 1955

Q. Are you Married?
A. Yes. Have been for 3 years.

Above: Patsy Cline's handwritten answers
to Treva Miller's questionnaire, 1955.

Top and bottom right: Cline gratefully obliged fans by posing
for photos and signing autographs.

Courtesy of Mario Munoz

gospel numbers. As Bradley later put it, "We'd try anything that might stick." Both artist and producer were hampered by the generally mediocre 4 Star songs Cline was required to record. Of the fifty-one masters she made for 4 Star, nineteen were songs co-credited to Bill McCall under his nom de plume "W. S. Stevenson." Most of the rest were written by songwriters who had little success in the music business. She released eighteen singles during her 4 Star years; only one was a hit.

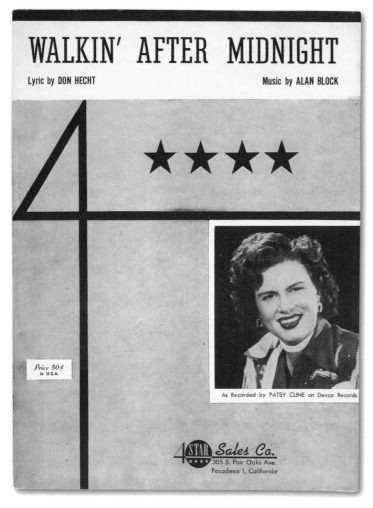

Sheet music for "Walkin' After Midnight."
Courtesy of the family of Patsy Cline

Decca would probably have given up on 4 Star's hillbilly pop singer, if not for that one magical hit. "Walkin' After Midnight" was written by Don Hecht and Alan Block, originally for Kay Starr. Starr's label, Capitol, had rejected the song, but Bill McCall got Hecht to unearth the number for Patsy Cline. McCall believed it had pop hit potential and insisted that Patsy record it. In a move that would become a pattern, she tried to reject it, saying, "It's nothin' but a little ol' pop song. I hate it." As a consolation prize, McCall allowed her to choose the B-side she wanted to record, "A Poor Man's Roses (or a Rich Man's Gold)."

"Walkin' After Midnight" was recorded in Nashville on November 8, 1956. In the hands of Bradley and his musicians, the bluesy song swings casually yet confidently. Also, it sounds simultaneously country and pop without being at all contrived. It didn't hurt that Hank Williams's former steel guitar player, Don Helms, contributed licks that would have sounded right at home on his boss's timeless recordings.

"Walkin' After Midnight" turned out to be Patsy's first hit, and a huge one at that. It received a big boost through television. On January 21, 1957, after failing two previous auditions in 1955 and 1956, she appeared as a contestant on CBS-TV's prime-time performing competition show, *Arthur Godfrey's Talent Scouts*. She was chosen as the night's winner, and the broadcast propelled her single to #2 on the country charts and #12 on the pop charts. The winning performance also gained her several more appearances on Godfrey's morning and evening TV programs, as well as network shows such as Alan Freed's ABC-TV telecast, *The Big Beat*.

Assisted by Decca executive Harry Silverstein, Cline displays her *Billboard* Award for Most Promising Country & Western Female Artist of 1957 at Nashville's 1957 DJ Convention. *Courtesy of Julie Fudge and Charlie Dick / Award photo by Bob Delevante*

Naturally, Bill McCall and Decca executives thought Patsy had made the pop breakthrough they had been hoping for. They scheduled her next two recording sessions—April 24 and 25, 1957—in New York. She recorded eight songs with vocal chorus singers for the first time, along with horns and other pop touches. However, none of them sold well, and subsequently she made her recordings in Nashville. After thirteen 4 Star sessions, eighteen singles (with only one hit in the bunch), and one album, Patsy Cline was released

from her contract on September 30, 1960. Her 4 Star royalty statement dated July 1, 1960, shows her in debt to 4 Star to the tune of $4,856.40 for unrecouped advances on royalties. The lone bright spot in her career at the time was gaining a slot in the Grand Ole Opry cast on January 9, 1960, a prize she had long coveted.

Owen Bradley, by then Decca's head of country A&R, made a fresh start with Patsy when she signed directly with

Continued on page 50

Owen Bradley and Patsy Cline in the studio, c. 1956.
Photo by Elmer Williams

Ray Walker

PATSY CLINE AND OWEN BRADLEY

"Owen saw the whole picture, and he knew it from listening to Patsy's voice and hearing the gutsy way she sang 'Walkin' After Midnight' and everything else that she had done. But he could see more in her than she dared see in herself....

"I've often thought that Owen Bradley had what we say a woman has: a sixth sense.... Just a hint of something out of the ordinary that you would do or say, or a certain feeling you would give, even in a conversation—he could translate that into music....

"From what we were told, they'd had some pretty stormy sessions about the music and the things to record. And it wasn't because they were being personal with each other, it's just that you've got this genius of Owen Bradley as a producer, and you've got that untold genius of a singer sitting there, who's just as gutsy with her life as Owen ever thought about being in his life, and both of them just as honest as they could be. See, that's the thing that kept them together....

"'I Fall to Pieces,' although you like the material, you're a little fearful of showing that emotion.... After that, she was not fearful of singing those songs anymore, the ballads.... She thought it had to be up-tempo. But when she started singing the ballads, she not only found a joy and a release in it, but she found out, 'Well, I can sing those.' And Owen Bradley was the miracle behind Patsy Cline."

Ray Walker, a stalwart of the Jordanaires vocal quartet since 1958, is a member of the Country Music Hall of Fame.

Decca Records in the fall of 1960 for an advance of $1,000. Now he could record her without restrictions on material. Bradley decided Patsy should record a combination of new country songs by Nashville's hottest young writers, pop standards, and well-known country songs from the recent past, such as the hits of Hank Williams. From this point Patsy's music took on the characteristics of what we now call the Nashville Sound: a hybrid country-pop style that Bradley and other country record producers hit upon to enlarge the genre's adult fan base. In place of fiddles and prominent steel guitars, Bradley increasingly backed her vocals with hushed choruses by the Jordanaires, restrained guitar work, and more prominent pop-style piano. By the time of her second Decca session, Bradley occasionally added violins, viola, and cello for good measure. Overall, Bradley's goal was to create a relaxed, accessible sound that could appeal to country and pop audiences alike.

It worked. He picked a hit for Patsy on her first Decca session, though once again she didn't want to record it. Hank Cochran and Harlan Howard had collaborated on a new song titled "I Fall to Pieces." When Owen Bradley called up one day for material, Cochran told him he had a new song that was "ambidextrous," meaning it could work for a man or a woman. Bradley tried the song on other singers on his roster—Roy Drusky and Brenda Lee—but they turned it down. By the time Bradley brought it to Patsy, she rejected it on the basis that other singers had found it lacking. Bradley didn't budge, though he allowed Patsy to choose whatever B-side she liked. He felt confident this song was a hit.

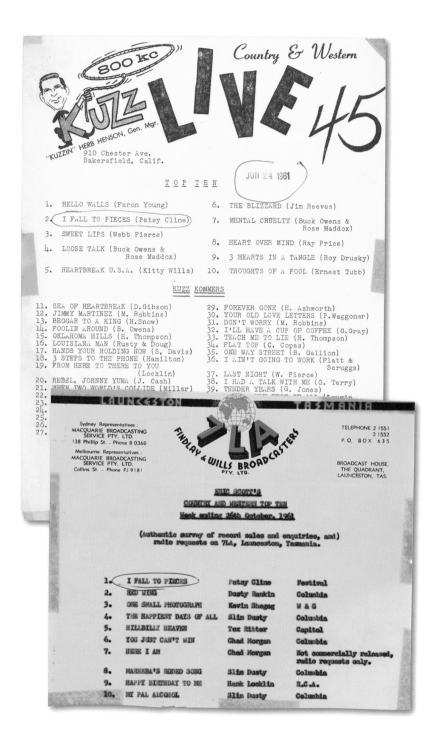

Cline saved mailings from radio broadcasters across the United States and overseas. These, from Bakersfield, California, DJ Herb Henson (top) and Findley & Wills Broadcasters in Launceston, Tasmania (bottom), document her hit "I Fall to Pieces." *Courtesy of the estate of Patsy Cline*

Recording at Nashville's Bradley Studios, c. 1956. Left to right: Owen Bradley, Patsy Cline, and Paul Cohen.
Photo by Elmer Williams / Business card courtesy of the family of Patsy Cline

Patsy Cline recorded "I Fall to Pieces" on November 16, 1960. The performance took shape with the rhythm section playing a standard country shuffle. But on top of that rhythmic foundation, Bradley reworked the shuffle's architecture. The track sets a distinct mood—Hank Garland's echo-treated guitar cascades, the Jordanaires hovering in the background like spirits of regret, Ben Keith's steel wafting in, Pig Robbins's piano showering delicate notes like so many teardrops, all propelled by an undeniably catchy shuffle rhythm. Above it all, Patsy's voice floats, forlorn and inconsolable. The song was a ballad of heartbreak, but it had a beat.

It took nine months and lots of radio promotion to do it, but in August 1961, Patsy Cline had her first hit in four

Continued on page 54

Patsy in Las Vegas

"When we first got to Las Vegas, I don't think Patsy wanted to go in the first place. I think she was scared. I drove out and got there. I took a couple of musicians. When we got there the first night, she just started crying. She wanted to go home. She didn't want to stay at all. I don't know whether she thought she wasn't prepared, or she'd heard so much about Vegas and all the big names out there and it scared her, or what, but she wasn't ready for it for some reason. Of course, after a couple of nights, there wasn't any problem.

"But the worst thing, the first week she started at two in the morning and worked till like six. At six o'clock in the morning, if you get one person sitting there—if you ain't got any—you put on a show just as if you had a full house. That was a bad scene, because at six o'clock in the morning, you ain't got any people. You'd maybe have a half dozen. Not being there and not knowing what's going on, she thought she wasn't drawing people. The next week, I think it started at eight o'clock at night and worked till two. Then the crowds were good.

"And of course, she got laryngitis and she couldn't sing. We had to play records backstage and she'd pantomime. It wasn't the first week. It seemed like it was in the middle. We were there thirty-five days. That was another thing. Part of the deal, you worked every day. You worked thirty-five days straight."

—Charlie Dick

Left: The Mint Theater, 1962.
Courtesy of Julie Fudge and Charlie Dick

Below Left: Patsy (in blonde wig), her mother, Hilda Hensley, and an unidentified man enjoying a Hank Thompson show at the Golden Nugget in Las Vegas, 1962.
Courtesy of Mario Munoz

Below: Outside the Mint Theater in Las Vegas, 1962.
Courtesy of Julie Fudge and Charlie Dick

Photo from personal collection of Hilda Hensley

years. It became her first #1 country hit, and a #12 pop chart maker as well. In the coming months, she would appear on *American Bandstand* and other national TV programs. The success of "I Fall to Pieces" bolstered Patsy's confidence in doing slower, more contemplative material. "I think I've found out who I am and what we've been looking for," Patsy told

APR • 62

Above: With the Jordanaires, 1962.
Left to right: Gordon Stoker,
Ray Walker, Patsy Cline, and
Neal Matthews Jr.

Right: Promotional match book.
Courtesy of Mario Munoz
Photo by Bob Delevante

Opposite: Sheet music for "Crazy," printed in England and distributed for Pamper Music by Acuff-Rose Publications' London office, misspelled Cline's last name.
Courtesy of Mario Munoz

Owen Bradley around this time. "We don't have to search for my identity anymore. This is it! We're doing it right."

Nevertheless, there would continue to be disagreements—sometimes heated—between Patsy and her producer about choice of material and approach. That was Patsy Cline's nature. "She argued with Owen almost any time when he would start playing the piano and we'd start running something down [rehearsing]," said Gordon Stoker. "She would have something about the song she didn't like that Owen was doing. Maybe she had been listening to the demo at home, and she had in her mind, maybe, how she wanted to record it.... My point: She was very headstrong, extremely headstrong.... She might as well have been fighting a brick wall. If Owen didn't want it that way, it wasn't going to be that way."

Decca released seven Patsy Cline singles while she was living. In marked contrast to her aimless 4 Star years, all of these singles made the charts, most of them placing high on both the country and pop ledgers. The two albums she released during these years, *Showcase* (1961) and *Sentimentally Yours* (1962), also sold well. But even though "I Fall to Pieces" had been a breakthrough success, it had not made the splash on the East Coast that Decca's executives had hoped for.

"Our people in New York said they couldn't get it on the New York stations," Owen Bradley told journalist Michael McCall. "They asked if we could make the next one a little less country. That's when we did 'Crazy.'"

PATSY CLINE
DECCA RECORDS
TV and RADIO STAR
•
Phone
MO. 2-1337
WINCHESTER, VA.

CRAZY

By WILLIE NELSON

Recorded by
PATSY KLINE
on BRUNSWICK Records

Acuff-Rose Publications Ltd.
50, NEW BOND STREET, LONDON, W.1
PAMPER MUSIC INC. TENNESSEE

12091

Made in England

2/-
NET

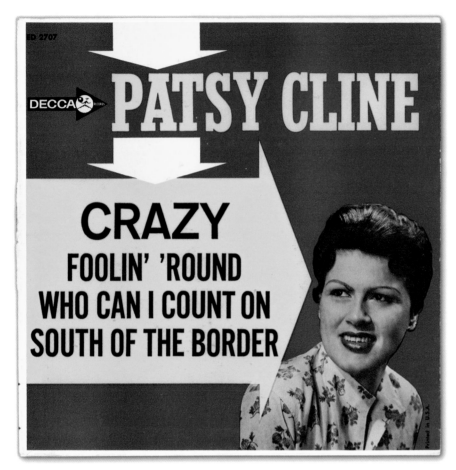

Extended play (EP) recording featuring "Crazy," 1962.
Courtesy of Julie Fudge

"Crazy" represents the zenith of Patsy Cline's success. It is her most covered song, the #1 jukebox hit of all time, her highest-charting pop hit at #9, and a #2 country hit as well. It too was a song Patsy did not want to record. Originally, she had hoped to record another song by the same writer, "Funny How Time Slips Away." The writer was Willie Nelson. But that song was on hold for one of her friends, Opry star Billy Walker. Songwriter Hank Cochran and Charlie Dick both urged Patsy to record "Crazy." Try as she might, Patsy couldn't warm up to this new Willie Nelson tune. On the demo recording, Willie phrased ahead of and behind the beat and sometimes almost spoke the lyric. Today it's become his trademark sound, but to Patsy Cline in 1961 it sounded like a bad record.

In contrast, Owen Bradley liked the song. It had the torchy, late-night quality he was after, and above all the lyric was right. Bradley was so certain "Crazy" could be a hit that he spent an entire four-hour session on it, which was unheard of in those days, when four songs in three hours was the session norm in Nashville. Even so, Patsy still couldn't get the vocal right. "I can't sing it like that, hoss," is what she told Bradley and the assembled musicians. Bradley told her she could come back and record her vocal later in an overdub, something she never did before or after, other than singing overdubbed harmony with herself.

It was sage advice. When she came back several days later—likely September 15, 1961, according to studio logbooks—she nailed the vocal in the first take. The record took off and remains a recording touchstone to this day.

With hits on the charts, Decca's New York executives soon demanded that Bradley record more material so the label could release Patsy Cline albums. "My company told me to make albums that would last ten years," Bradley told Bob Millard. "What we did was this: You put songs in there that were gonna last." So Bradley worked with Patsy to choose a number of pop and country standards and well-loved

Continued on page 60

Looking glamorous, c. 1957.

Right: Cocktail gown and rhinestone earrings
worn by Patsy Cline.
Earrings courtesy of the family of Patsy Cline
Earrings and dress, photos by Bob Delevante

Carnegie Hall

In 1961, Patsy Cline joined a troupe of Grand Ole Opry stars at New York City's prestigious Carnegie Hall for a concert benefiting the city's Musicians Aid Society.

Onstage at Carnegie Hall, November 29, 1961.
Courtesy of Mario Munoz

Right: Ticket stub and advertising flyer from the Carnegie Hall concert.
Courtesy of Mario Munoz

CARNEGIE HALL
57th Street at 7th Avenue
GRAND OLE OPRY
Musicians' Aid Society, Inc
SEAT 26
NOV. 29 1961
WEDNESDAY EVENING
8:30 P. M.
PARQUET
ROW A
Admission $5.00

WSM Invites You to a Night at the
GRAND OLE OPRY

The artists appearing here tonight have traveled from Nashville's Grand Ole Opry to contribute their talent in support of the efforts of The Musicians Aid Society of New York.

FARON YOUNG

JIM REEVES

MARTY ROBBINS

BILL MONROE

PATSY CLINE

JORDANAIRES

GRANDPA JONES

MINNIE PEARL

T. TOMMY CUTRER
Master of Ceremonies

Featuring
TOMMY JACKSON and
BEN SMATHERS AND THE
STONY MOUNTAIN CLOGGERS

Right: Grand Ole Opry performers accept the keys to the city on the steps of New York's City Hall, before their November 29, 1961, Carnegie Hall performance. Left to right: Grandpa Jones, Minnie Pearl, Faron Young, Bill Monroe, and Patsy Cline.
Photo by Les Leverett

Lower right: Key to New York City, given to Patsy Cline on behalf of Mayor Robert F. Wagner on November 29, 1961.
Courtesy of Charlie Dick / Photo by Bob Delevante

Left: Patsy Cline, Randy Hughes, and *Nashville Banner* columnist Red O'Donnell (seated, far left) wait to depart New York's LaGuardia Airport following the Carnegie Hall concert.
Photo by Les Leverett

Below: Telegram to Patsy Cline from well-wishers on the day of her Carnegie Hall appearance.
Courtesy of the family of Patsy Cline

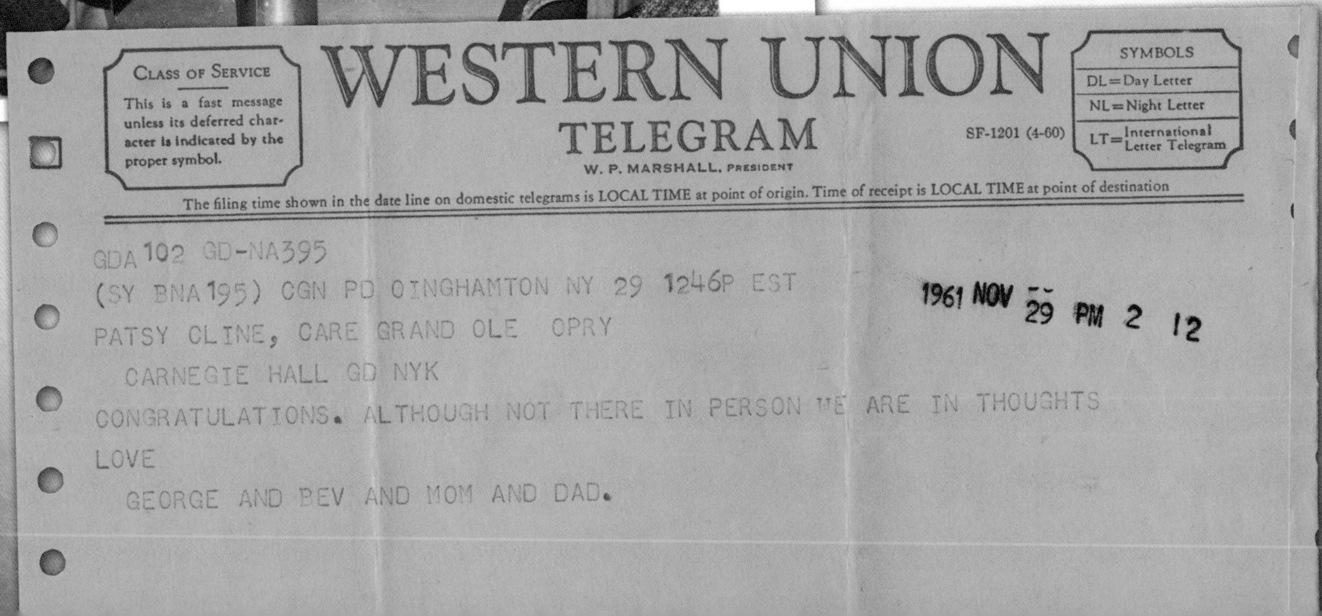

CLASS OF SERVICE
This is a fast message unless its deferred character is indicated by the proper symbol.

WESTERN UNION
TELEGRAM
W. P. MARSHALL, PRESIDENT

SF-1201 (4-60)

SYMBOLS
DL = Day Letter
NL = Night Letter
LT = International Letter Telegram

The filing time shown in the date line on domestic telegrams is LOCAL TIME at point of origin. Time of receipt is LOCAL TIME at point of destination

GDA 102 GD-NA395
(SY BNA195) CGN PD OINGHAMTON NY 29 1246P EST   1961 NOV 29 PM 2 12
PATSY CLINE, CARE GRAND OLE OPRY
    CARNEGIE HALL GD NYK
CONGRATULATIONS. ALTHOUGH NOT THERE IN PERSON WE ARE IN THOUGHTS
LOVE
    GEORGE AND BEV AND MOM AND DAD.

TV Guide entry and screen still from Patsy's appearance on ABC's *American Bandstand*, 1962.

Courtesy of Mario Munoz

songs. Craftily, Bradley had her record several songs that had previously been successful as both country and pop records for other artists: "San Antonio Rose" (Bob Wills, Bing Crosby), "Have You Ever Been Lonely" (Ernest Tubb, pop bandleader Ted Lewis), "South of the Border" (Gene Autry, Frank Sinatra), "You Belong to Me" (Pee Wee King, Jo Stafford), "Anytime" (Eddy Arnold, Eddie Fisher), and "Your Cheatin' Heart" (Hank Williams, Rosemary Clooney). Still, Patsy resisted some of these ideas.

In August 1961, during the sessions for her *Showcase* album, she wrote to friend Marie Flynt: "I had 21 songs picked for the album plus 7 new ones for 4 singles to come out of and that dam [sic] Owen Bradley turned down everything except 2 out of 7 for the singles and 4 for the album out of 12. I could spit dust I'm so mad. And he wants to put violins (you heard me) on my new session. Still trying to get me to go pop. And I'll die & walk out before I'll go all the way pop."

Gradually, as sales picked up and her career took off, Patsy began to accept that she could be on the pop charts as well as the country charts, and her country audience would still accept her. At the annual Country Music Disc Jockey Convention in Nashville in November 1962, she was named *Billboard*'s Favorite Female Country & Western Artist (as voted by country DJs) for the second year in a row, and she earned similar honors from the other music trade magazines: *Cash Box*, *Music Reporter*, and *Music Vendor*.

On February 26, 1962, she wrote Marie Flynt again, saying, "I finally got my record check and don't let anyone else know but I've just got to tell you. It was twenty-three thousand dollars. I can't get used to it yet. First I cried, then I laughed, then I prayed & thanked God, then I cried & laughed some more. Boy! What a feeling."

Patsy Cline's 1962 *Billboard* Award for Favorite Female Country & Western Artist, as voted by country disc jockeys.
Courtesy of Charlie Dick / Photo by Bob Delevante

Small wonder that Patsy Cline was elated by her record royalties. She lived a hard life. Her father may have sexually abused her, and he left her and her family destitute. She had to work night and day as a teenager to help provide for her family. She didn't enjoy consistent hit records till the last two years of her life. Even her romantic life was often tempestuous. Her first husband's jealousy of her career led to divorce. She and her second husband, Charlie Dick, fought frequently, and she even went so far as to file for divorce in July 1962, though she relented and they reconciled, as she recounted at the time in letters and conversations with her friends.

According to biographer Margaret Jones, Patsy Cline was involved in two automobile crashes that sent her to the hospital. Little information has been uncovered on the first one, purportedly in Mississippi in 1959 when Patsy was touring. The second car accident is well documented.

In June 1961, just as her career was finally catching fire with the success of "I Fall to Pieces," she nearly died. On Wednesday, June 14, Patsy's twenty-one-year-old brother John was driving her in the Madison suburb of Nashville in a rainstorm, when a car hit them head-on in its attempt to pass another vehicle. As Patsy later told a concert audience: "It broke my hip—dislocated it, and broke my right arm and cut my face up a little bit." Actually, the injuries were much worse than that. When brought to

Continued on page 66

Above: Sympathy letter to Patsy from John Kenworthy, general manager of Charlotte, North Carolina, radio station WKTC, following her 1961 car wreck.
Courtesy of the family of Patsy Cline

Opposite: Outtake from the photo shoot for Cline's album *Sentimentally Yours*, 1962.

Roy Drusky

"SHE WAS A VERY HONEST PERSON"

"We worked a deal somewhere up in the North where the guy ran off with all the money—Patsy Cline and, I think, the Willis Brothers, and it seems like Bill Anderson and myself. I'm not sure Bill was on it, but it seems like it. And the promoter left with all the money before the show. It was a pretty good crowd in this theater. We were all hot you know, and nobody was gonna work. And Patsy was the one that finally said, 'Well, it's not these people's fault. They came here to see a show, and it's not their fault this bum ran off with all the money.' She said, 'I don't know about y'all, but I'm gonna go out here and do 'em a show.'... So we all went out and did a show for 'em.

"But that's kind of the kind of girl she was, you know. She was right. It wasn't the people's fault, and they had paid in good faith to see us. We were there. And had we left, that wouldn't have been fair to them, either. Two wrongs don't make a right, so we did the show after Patsy said, 'I'm gonna go out there and do these people a show, 'cause it's not their fault.' She was a very honest person."

Roy Drusky (1930–2004) starred on the Grand Ole Opry from 1959 until his death.

At the Riverside Ballroom, Phoenix, Arizona, 1962.
Photo by Johnny Franklin / Courtesy of Mario Munoz

Madison General Hospital, doctors rated her as "critical." She needed three pints of blood, had sustained a jagged gash across her forehead requiring stitches, and had to remain in the hospital in traction for a month. Over subsequent months she would require repeated plastic surgery to repair her forehead, and for the rest of her career she tended to wear bangs or headbands to hide the scars. Released from the hospital on July 17, she returned to the stage of the Grand Ole Opry in a wheelchair. She didn't perform again till July 29, and then it was sitting on a stool, with crutches.

And yet Patsy was soon back on the road, performing coast to coast. On November 29, 1961, she played Carnegie Hall with a Grand Ole Opry troupe including Jim Reeves, Minnie Pearl, Bill Monroe, Grandpa Jones, Marty Robbins, the Jordanaires, and Faron Young. In June 1962, she appeared at the Hollywood Bowl on a bill with Johnny Cash, Don Gibson, George Jones, and Leroy Van Dyke. Later that same year, she landed her first (and last) Las Vegas casino engagement, from November 23 to December 28.

In early 1963, Patsy Cline's prospects appeared bright. She was touring regularly, her asking price was around $1,000 per show, and her latest single, "Leavin' on Your Mind," was approaching the country Top Ten and making inroads on the pop charts. She and Owen Bradley were considering material for her next album. They planned to call it *Faded Love*, and the photograph intended for the

Owen Bradley, Randy Hughes, and Patsy Cline, early 1960s.

cover captured her in soft, misty focus wearing a gold dress against a matte gold background. For this album, she was planning to record new songs such as "Lock, Stock and Teardrops" by her friend Roger Miller and "We Could" by the husband-wife songwriting team of Boudleaux and Felice Bryant. Owen Bradley said that he and Patsy were even considering recording an album of Broadway show tunes for future release.

None of that came to pass. One month after her last recording session, she traveled to Kansas City to do a benefit performance for the family of DJ "Cactus" Jack Call, who had died in a car crash and lacked insurance. Joining her on the bill were Grand Ole Opry stars George Jones, Billy Walker, Dottie West, Cowboy Copas, and Hawkshaw Hawkins. The show raised $3,000—a large sum in those days—for the Call family. Patsy was suffering from the flu during her performance, but by all accounts it went well, and she looked elegant in her white, long-sleeved sheath dress. She closed to a standing ovation and told the audience, "I love you all."

On March 5, 1963, on the return flight back to Nashville, the small Piper Comanche flown by Patsy's manager,

Randy Hughes, crashed in a rainstorm in rural Camden, Tennessee. Also aboard were Cowboy Copas and Hawkshaw Hawkins. There were no survivors.

In the years after her death, Patsy Cline's stature has only grown. The list of female artists who have recorded her songs or acknowledged her influence reads like a who's who of American music. Linda Ronstadt. k.d. lang. Brenda Lee. Tammy Wynette. Loretta Lynn. Dottie West. Barbara Mandrell. Reba McEntire. Trisha Yearwood. Sara Evans. Rosanne Cash. Diana Krall. Fiona Apple. Cat Power. Neko Case. Madeleine Peyroux. Martina McBride. Lee Ann Womack. LeAnn Rimes. Terri Clark. K. T. Oslin. Shelby Lynne. Amy Grant. Mandy Barnett. Norah Jones. Patty Griffin. The list goes on and on.

Continued on page 70

Program from a benefit show for the family of DJ "Cactus" Jack Call, and what proved to be Patsy Cline's final performance.

Courtesy of Guy Cesario, Bill Cox, Phillip Martin, Theresa Shalaby, and C. Mark Willix.

WSM
GRAND OLE OPRY

BENEFIT SHOW

"CACTUS"
JACK CALL

"CACTUS"
JACK CALL

MEMORIAL BUILDING
KANSAS CITY, KANSAS

March 3, 1963

Ray Walker

PATSY'S LAST WORDS AT THE RYMAN

"She knew she had this charity thing to do. She had hugged us all, and she had told us she'd see us the next trip in. It'd be a little bit. And she put on this full-length black mink coat. She got this coat on, and she's picking up her purse, and here she was going....So I was more toward the back there, toward the back door, and I said, 'Patsy, honey,' and she turned around. I said, 'Be careful, baby. We sure love you.' And she was just starting to go down those back steps at the Ryman, the back entrance there, and she stopped. And she didn't turn her body, but she flipped the collar up on that coat and pulled it around that pretty little face of hers, and she looked over that shoulder and just kind of slung that head at me, kinda cocky-like. Held her head back, and she said, 'Honey, I've been in two bad ones. The third one'll be a charm, or it'll kill me.' And then she did this little strut down those steps, you know. She was just kinda like, 'Well, just look at me. Ain't I something?' And she waved and walked on out, went to her car. And those are the last words she said in the Ryman Auditorium. She never got back there."

Ray Walker joined the Jordanaires vocal quartet in 1958. The group was elected to the Country Music Hall of Fame in 2001.

Opposite: At the Grand Ole Opry, Ryman Auditorium, 1961.

"Patsy was way ahead of her times," Owen Bradley told journalist Susan Nadler. "She was the first country girl in the fifties with a smooth polished voice—what she really had was a pop voice in a country music head. Until Patsy, no country female singer dared being smooth—they were all rough. Patsy opened the way for gals like Tammy Wynette to be accepted."

Patsy Cline's life had more than its share of tragedy and heartache. Nothing came easy to her, except singing. Yet on balance her life is a testament to the power of the human spirit. Time and again, she encountered staggering obstacles, and she overcame them. In life, many people are talented. The ones we remember are the ones who persevered.

Her gravesite can be found in Winchester, in Shenandoah Memorial Park. The simple bronze plaque reads:

VIRGINIA H. [PATSY CLINE] DICK – 1932–1963
"DEATH CANNOT KILL WHAT NEVER DIES."

Underneath that line is the single word "LOVE." Her passionate love for music lives on through the ages, and her gift rewards all who listen as she sang— with an open heart. ∎

Above right: Patsy's daughter, Julie, accepts her mother's posthumous 1963 *Cashbox* award for Most Programmed Female Vocalist, Country & Western, Grand Ole Opry Birthday Celebration, Nashville, November 1963.
Photo by Les Leverett / Courtesy of Julie Fudge and Charlie Dick

Opposite: A fan's snapshot of Patsy, taken at her final show in Kansas City, Kansas, March 3, 1961.
Photo by Johnny Franklin / Courtesy of Mario Munoz

Nashville Banner.

Nashville's Oldest Newspaper

VOL. LXXXVI, NO. 263

LONG MAY OUR LAND BE BRIGHT WITH FREEDOM'S HOLY LIGHT: PROTECT US BY THY MIGHT, GREAT GOD, OUR KING

NASHVILLE, TENN., WED. AFTERNOON, MAR. 6, 1963

40 PAGES

Founded April 10, 1876

PRICE: TEN CENTS

4 OPRY STARS DIE IN CRASH

Plane Debris Yields Bodies At Camden

By LARRY BRINTON and CLAY HARGIS

Camden—The remains of four country music personalities, including three nationally-known Grand Old Opry stars, were found this morning in the scattered bits of a private plane which crashed in rugged woodlands near here.

The victims were assumed to be Patsy Cline, Cowboy Copas, Hawkshaw Hawkins and Randy Hughes, believed pilot of the ill-fated aircraft.

The wreckage was discovered about 6 a.m. after a night-long search by highway patrol, Civil Defense and local officers.

Parts of the yellow plane and bits of human flesh were scattered over a 60-yard area a mile off Highway 70 about three miles west of Camden. The wreckage was between the highway and a ranger tower, which had served as a base of operations for searchers.

Civil Defense official Dean Brewer, asked whether all four bodies had been located, replied: "There's not enough to count . . . They're all in small pieces."

The plane left Dyersburg about 6 p.m. Tuesday for a flight to Nashville. The entertainers had been in Kansas City, Kan., for a benefit performance for the late Cactus Jack Call, a disc jockey.

Sam Webb, whose farm is near the dense woodland, said he saw a plane circling his home about 7 p.m. and that it was "revving up its motor . . . going fast and then slow, like it was attempting to climb."

Webb said the plane left his sight and then he heard something "like it struck the tops of some

MATCHES **COLORTONE**
RAINBOW ENVELOPES

Fredericksburg Va. Mary Washington Hospital Room 194

COLOR
TONE

Rainbow Tablet

25¢

NO. 2908

Handwritten autobiography,
composed by Patsy Cline,
c. 1962.
Courtesy of the family of Patsy Cline

Born In Winchester, Va
~~Shenadooh Valley~~ Born Va Patterson Hensley
Started tap danceing & won a contest
at age 4 & 5
At age 15 started singing with
Sammy Moss at W.I.N.C.
Sang at school show churches & so on
Started singing in 1952 with a local
band over radio station WEP.M. in
Martinsburg W. Va. & worked Brunswick
Moose Club in Brunswick Md every Sat
nite for 3 years.
Then Jimmy Dean heard me on some
of the stations.
Called me to do some shows with
him on Town & Country Time in Wash,
In 1953 I got a recording contract with
4 Star Records & got married. First Hubby
was named Cline.
Stayed with Dean for 3 years and
worked with Grey back & forth between
sessions.
Jimmy Dickeons & Walley ~~Fowler~~ & E.
Tubb was the friends who told the

Opry people I could sing.

In 1955 I tried with a local band for Godfree Talent Scout.

In 1956. I tried again. Was too young to be out on my own.

In 1957 I tried again, got called + Monday Jan 21st 1957 I won with Walkin After Mid. which sold 1 million + 1/4. records to date. Stayed 2 yrs.

In 1957 I remarried Charles A Dick.

In 1958 I had a baby girl named Julia Simadore Dick while Charles was doing 2 years in Ft Bragg N.C. with Army.

After Army we spent one more year back in Va then Sept. 1959 moved back to Nashville. Four mos later I joined the Opry.

In Jan 1961 I had a boy Allan Randolph Dick.

Then 1961 June 14 I had I Fall To Pieces go to No1. & had a head on wreck was in hospital for 1 mos.

Toured the country on Cruches for a while. Got over 400 a letters + cards

Then next record was Crazy + on Nov 3 + 5 was chosen

Queen of C & W. music + No 1. girl singer
for 1961. + had 2 hit songs
1961. I Fall To Pieces

Hank Cochran + Harland Howard
writers of I Fall To Pieces —

(Crazy was written by Willie Nelson.

Did the Dick Clark show on Nov 8th.

On Nov 29th along with Minnie
Pearl Jim Reeves Faron Young Marty
Robbins Grand pa Jones, Jordanaires
Bill Monroe Tommy Jackson + Stoney
mountain Cloggers we play to a packed
+ standing audience in Carnegie Hall
N. Y City.

Crazy + Pieces have both become #1.
in C + W. field + newest release is
"She's Got You" + Album called
"Showcase" #1. seller in albums for
Decca.

Ham worked such shows as
Big Beat in N. Y. Hodjee show,
Howard Miller show in Chicago
Philip Morris show, Town Hall Party

Sources

BOOKS

Bufwack, Mary A., and Robert K. Oermann. *Finding Her Voice: Women in Country Music, 1800–2000*. Nashville: The Country Music Foundation Press & Vanderbilt University Press, 2003.

Country Music Foundation. *Country: The Music and the Musicians: From the Beginnings to the '90s*. Edited by Alan Axelrod, Susan Costello, and Paul Kingsbury. Rev. ed. New York: Abbeville Press, 1994.

Dawidoff, Nicholas. *In the Country of Country: People and Places in American Music*. New York: Pantheon Books, 1997.

Dean, Jimmy, and Donna Meade Dean. *Thirty Years of Sausage, Fifty Years of Ham: Jimmy Dean's Own Story*. New York: Berkley Books, 2004.

Hagan, Chet. *Country Music Legends in the Hall of Fame*. Nashville: Thomas Nelson Publishers and Country Music Foundation Press, 1982.

Hazen, Cindy, and Mike Freeman. *Love Always, Patsy: Patsy Cline's Letters to a Friend*. New York: Berkley Books, 1999.

Jensen, Joli. *The Nashville Sound: Authenticity, Commercialization, and Country Music*. Nashville and London: The Country Music Foundation Press & Vanderbilt University Press, 1998.

Jones, Margaret. *Patsy: The Life and Times of Patsy Cline*. New York: HarperCollins Publishers, 1994.

Kingsbury, Paul, Michael McCall, and John W. Rumble, eds. *The Encyclopedia of Country Music*. Rev. ed. Oxford: Oxford University Press, 2012.

Kosser, Michael. *How Nashville Became Music City, U.S.A.: 50 Years of Music Row*. Milwaukee: Hal Leonard, 2006.

Mansfield, Brian. *Remembering Patsy*. Nashville: Rutledge Hill Press, 2002.

Nassour, Ellis. *Patsy Cline*. New York: Tower Publications, 1981.

Profiles in History Presents the Hilda Hensley Patsy Cline Auction, December 19, 2002. Auction catalog. Source of Marie Flynt letters.

Whitburn, Joel. *Top Country Singles, 1944–2001*. Menomonee Falls, Wisconsin: Record Research, 2002.

Whitburn, Joel. *Top Pop Singles, 1955–2002*. Menomonee Falls, Wisconsin: Record Research, 2003.

ARTICLES

Burnes, Brian. "To Patsy with Love and Regret: A Trip to Kansas City 30 Years Ago Led Legendary Singer to Her Death." *Kansas City Star*, March 2, 1993.

Gerome, John. "Patsy Cline's Legacy Lives 40 Years After Her Death." Associated Press, March 5, 2003.

Korpan, Steve. "Woman Killed in Car Smash." *Nashville Tennessean*. June 15, 1961.

McCall, Michael. "Owen Bradley's 'Invigorating Therapy.'" *Nashville Banner*, June 9, 1988.

Millard, Bob. "Patsy Cline: Owen Bradley Remembers." *Goldmine*, December 4, 1987.

Morley, Steve. "Backtracking: Patsy Cline's 'Crazy' Session. *Nashville Monitor*, May 15, 1990, 1–17.

Gantry, Susan Nadler. "A Portrait of Patsy Cline." *Country Music*, May 1979, 64–66.

"Owen Bradley Seeking the New; Views the Old." *Billboard*, August 7, 1961.

LINER NOTES

Kienzle, Rich. Liner notes to *Patsy Cline: The Birth of a Star*. Razor & Tie RE 2108-2 (1996).

Kingsbury, Paul. Liner notes to *Patsy Cline: Live at the Cimarron Ballroom*. MCA MCAD-11579 (1997).

Kingsbury, Paul. Liner notes to *Patsy Cline: The Patsy Cline Collection*. Four-CD box. MCA MCAD4-10421 (1991).

Kingsbury, Paul. Liner notes to *Remembering Patsy Cline*. MCA 088 170 297-2 (2003).

Orr, Jay, and Don Roy. Liner notes to *Patsy Cline: 12 Greatest Hits*. MCA MCAD-12 (1988).

Pugh, Ronnie. Liner notes to *Patsy Cline: Live at the Opry*. MCA MCAD-42142 (1988).

INTERVIEWS

Bradley, Harold. Interviewed by John Rumble: May 14, 1991.

Bradley, Harold. Interviewed by Paul Kingsbury: May 5, 2002.

Bradley, Harold; Ray Edenton; Buddy Harman; Bob Moore. Interviewed together by Paul Kingsbury and John Rumble: May 17, 1991.

Cannon, Sarah (Minnie Pearl). Interviewed by Paul Kingsbury: May 1991.

Cochran, Hank. Interviewed by John Rumble: July 3, 1991.

Dick, Charlie. Interviewed by Paul Kingsbury and John Rumble: June 28, 1991.

Drusky, Roy. Interviewed by John Rumble: June 17, 1991.

Emery, Ralph. Interviewed by John Rumble: May 28, 1991.

Haddock, Durwood. Interviewed by Paul Kingsbury: June 1991.

Hamilton, George IV. Interviewed by Paul Kingsbury and John Rumble: June 27, 1991.

Helms, Don. Interviewed by John Rumble: May 29, 1991.

Howard, Jan. Interviewed by John Rumble: May 23, 1991.

Howard, Harlan. Interviewed by John Rumble: June 25, 1991.

Lynn, Loretta. Interviewed by Ralph Emery: 1968.

Miller, Roger. Interviewed by John Rumble: June 27, 1991.

Stoker, Gordon. Interviewed by Paul Kingsbury and John Rumble: June 13, 1991.

Turner, Grant. Interviewed by Paul Kingsbury: May 1991.

Walker, Ray. Interviewed by John Rumble: July 1, 1991.

ARTIFACTS

Research for both the exhibit and this book drew upon a number of rare and special sources, including a handwritten autobiography Cline prepared in 1962. She also made undated, handwritten notes about her figure on a paper tablet, and kept a sizable scrapbook. These items, in addition to important artifacts, photos, clippings, posters, and other materials, were loaned by the family of Patsy Cline. Many similar sources also were loaned by Mario Munoz. Others loaning significant items include Guy Cesario, Bill Cox, Charlie Dick, Julie Fudge, Judy Sue Huyett-Kemf (representing Celebrating Patsy Cline), Wayne Lensing (of Historic Auto Attractions), Philip Martin, the Patsy Cline Partnership, Theresa Shalaby, Jimmy Walker, and C. Mark Willix.

Suggested Books, CDs, and Video

BOOKS

Bufwack, Mary A., and Robert K. Oermann. *Finding Her Voice: Women in Country Music, 1800–2000*. Nashville: The Country Music Foundation Press & Vanderbilt University Press, 2003.

Country Music Foundation. *Country: The Music and the Musicians: From the Beginnings to The '90s*. Edited by Alan Aexlrod, Susan Costello, and Paul Kingsbury. Rev. ed. New York: Abbeville Press, 1994.

Dawidoff, Nicholas. *In the Country of Country: People and Places in American Music*. New York: Pantheon Books, 1997.

Dean, Jimmy, and Donna Meade Dean. *Thirty Years of Sausage, Fifty Years of Ham: Jimmy Dean's Own Story*. New York: Berkley Books, 2004.

Hazen, Cindy, and Mike Freeman. *Love Always, Patsy: Patsy Cline's Letters to a Friend*. New York: Berkley Books, 1999.

Jensen, Joli. *The Nashville Sound: Authenticity, Commercialization, and Country Music*. Nashville and London: The Country Music Foundation Press & Vanderbilt University Press, 1998.

Jones, Margaret. *Patsy: The Life and Times of Patsy Cline*. New York: HarperCollins Publishers, 1994.

Mansfield, Brian. *Remembering Patsy*. Nashville: Rutledge Hill Press, 2002.

Nassour, Ellis. *Patsy Cline*. New York: Tower Publications, 1981.

CDs

Cline, Patsy. *The Birth of a Star*. Razor & Tie RE 2108-2 (1996).

Cline, Patsy. *Live at the Cimarron Ballroom*. MCA MCAD-11579 (1997).

Cline, Patsy. *Live at the Opry*. MCA MCAD-42142 (1988).

Cline, Patsy. *The Patsy Cline Collection*. Four-CD box. MCA MCAD4-10421 (1991).

Cline, Patsy. *12 Greatest Hits*. MCA MCAD-12 (1988).

Starr, Kay. *Capitol Collectors Series*. Capitol CDP 7 94080 2 (1991).

Starr, Kay. *The RCA Years*. Collectors Choice Music CCM059-2 (1998).

Various Artists. *Remembering Patsy Cline*. MCA 088 170 297-2 (2003).

VIDEO

Cline, Patsy. *Sweet Dreams Still: The Anthology*. MPI Video (2005).

Pink marble lighter and cigarette jar belonging to Patsy Cline.
Courtesy of the family of Patsy Cline
Photo by Bob Delevante

Roger Miller
"SOME GOOD MEMORIES"

"She liked to come to Tootsie's with Charlie. We'd have a few beers, laugh, and play music. We usually wound up at somebody's house after Tootsie's closed. It would close around midnight. Then we'd go out to somebody's house and sing all night. We had some great times and made some good memories.

"She loved to laugh. She told a lot of dirty jokes. She liked to howl and laugh. She had a good soul and a good heart. She was a really good person, a person you wanted to have in your corner."

Singer, songwriter, recording artist, and TV star Roger Miller (1936–92) was elected to the Country Music Hall of Fame in 1995.